PhotoSecrets
TAJ MAHAL

A Photographer's Guide

By
Andrew Hudson

📷 Gallery

📷 Gallery by Time of Day

Dawn

Sunrise

Morning

Noon

Afternoon

Sunset

Dusk

Anytime

📣 Acclaim for PhotoSecrets

🏆 Grand Prize in the National Self-Published Book Awards
🏆 Benjamin Franklin Award for Best First Book

"Impressive in its presentation and abundance of material."
—National Geographic Traveler

"PhotoSecrets books are an invaluable resource for photographers."
—Nikon School of Photography

"One of the best travel photography books we've ever seen."
—Minolta

"Guides you to the most visually distinctive places to explore with your camera."
—Outdoor Photographer

"This could be one of the most needed travel books ever published!"
—San Francisco Bay Guardian

"The most useful travel guides for anyone with a camera."
—Shutterbug's Outdoor and Nature Photography

"Many professional photographers employ the services of full-time location scouts; Andrew Hudson may have put a lot of those folks out of work."
—Shutterbug

"Takes the guesswork out of shooting."
—American Way (American Airlines)

© Copyright

> *"One of the great things about books is sometimes there are some fantastic pictures."*
> — George W. Bush

> *"'And what is the use of a book,' thought Alice 'without pictures or conversations?'"*
> — Alice's Adventures in Wonderland, by Lewis Carroll

🖼 Photos

Thank you to the many talented photographers that generously made their photos available. Photos distributed by the following:

🖒 **Flickr**. Various licenses as noted, such as Creative Commons Attribution (CC BY).

🖒 **Shutterstock**. Images used under license from Shutterstock.com.

🖒 **Wikimedia and Wikipedia**. Various licenses as noted, such as Creative Commons Attribution (CC BY).

© Copyright

✦ Disclaimer

The information provided within this book is for general informational purposes only. Some information may be inadvertently incorrect, or may be incorrect in the source material, or may have changed since publication, this includes GPS (Global Positioning System) / WGS 84 (World Geodetic System, 1984) coordinates, addresses, location titles, descriptions, Web links, and photo credits. The publisher and author cannot accept responsibility for any consequences arising from the use of this book. There are no representations or warranties, express or implied, about the completeness, accuracy, reliability, suitability or availability with respect to the information, products, services, images, or graphics contained in this book for any purpose. Any use of this information is at your own risk.

For corrections, please email me at ahudson@photosecrets.com.

Table of Contents

Front matter 2
   Gallery 2
      by Rank 2
      by Time 3
   Copyright 6
   Contents 8
   Foreword 9
      About Bob Krist 10
   Welcome 11
      About Andrew Hudson 12
   About PhotoSecrets 13
   Maps 14
      Map of Taj Mahal 14
      Map of Entrance Forecourt 15
      Map of Paradise Garden 16
      Map of Riverfront Terrace 17
      Map of Yamuna River 18
   Introduction 19
      at a Glance 19
      Introduction 20
Views 22
   Entrance Forecourt 23
      Great Gate 23
         East gallery detail 25
         Ceiling 27
         Framed by doorway 28
      East Gate and cloisters 30
         East Gate corridor 32
      West Gate 35
         Interior 35
      Entrance well 36
   Paradise Garden 37
      Classic 37

sunrise 37

morning 38

Reflection 40

noon 42

afternoon 44

Grass 46

West 46

East 48

Pavilion 49

View of View of Great Gate 50

View of View of Mosque 52

Riverfront Terrace 54

View 54

at sunrise 54

at morning 55

at afternoon 56

Close 58

corner 58

sunset 60

side 61

top 63

Tomb 65

Details 65

art 65

inlay 67

Tombs in crypt 68

Mosque 69

Interior 69

Framed arch 71

silhouette 74

Photographer 76

Jawab 77

Interior 77

View of View of Great Gate 79

View of View of Mosque 81

View of northwest octagonal tower 82

Yamuna 83

  River 83

    northeast 83

      sunrise 83

      sunset 85

      boat 86

      bike 87

    north 88

      vertical 88

      sunset 90

    northwest 91

      dawn 91

      afternoon 92

        Cows 94

      sunset 95

      at dusk 97

Moonlight Garden 99

  View 101

from Agra Fort 102

Index 104

PhotoSecrets Taj Mahal

✒ Foreword

By Bob Krist

A GREAT TRAVEL photograph, like a great news photograph, requires you to be in the right place at the right time to capture that special moment. Professional photographers have a short-hand phrase for this: "F8 and be there."

There are countless books that can help you with photographic technique, the "F8" portion of that equation. But until now, there's been little help for the other, more critical portion of that equation, the "be there" part. To find the right spot, you had to expend lots of time and shoe leather to essentially re-invent the wheel.

In my career as a professional travel photographer, well over half my time on location is spent seeking out the good angles. Andrew Hudson's PhotoSecrets does all that legwork for you, so you can spend your time photographing instead of wandering about. It's like having a professional location scout in your camera bag. I wish I had one of these books for every city I photograph.

PhotoSecrets can help you capture the most beautiful sights with a minimum of hassle and a maximum of enjoyment. So grab your camera, find your favorite PhotoSecrets spots, and "be there!"

Bob Krist

About Bob Krist

BOB KRIST has photographed assignments for *National Geographic, National Geographic Traveler, Travel/Holiday, Smithsonian,* and *Islands.* He won "Travel photographer of the Year" from the Society of American Travel Writers in 1994, 2007, and 2008.

For *National Geographic,* Bob has led round-the-world tours and a traveling lecture series. His book *In Tuscany* with Frances Mayes spent a month on *The New York Times'* bestseller list and his how-to book *Spirit of Place* was hailed by *American photographer* magazine as "the best book about travel photography we've ever read."

The parents of three sons, Bob and his wife live in New Hope, Pennsylvania.

THANK YOU for reading PhotoSecrets. As a fellow fan of travel and photography, I hope this guide will help you quickly find the most visually stunning places, and come home with equally stunning photographs.

PhotoSecrets is designed to show you all the best sights. Flick through, see the classic views, and use them as a departure point for your own creations. Get composition ideas, lighting tips, and a brief history. It'll be like travelling with a location scout and a pro-photographer by your side.

Now, start exploring — and take lots of photos!

Andrew Hudson

About Andrew Hudson

ORIGINALLY an engineer, Andrew Hudson started PhotoSecrets in 1995. His first book won the Benjamin Franklin Award for Best First Book and his second won the Grand Prize in the National Self-Published Book Awards.

Andrew has published 15 nationally-distributed photography books. He has photographed assignments for *Macy's*, *Martha Stewart Living Omnimedia*, *Men's Health* and *Seventeen*, and been a location scout for *Nikon*. His photos and articles have appeared in *Alaska Airlines*, *National Geographic Traveler*, *Shutterbug Outdoor and Nature photography*, *Where*, and *Woman's World*.

Andrew has a degree in Computer Engineering from Manchester University and a certificate in copyright law from Harvard Law School. Born in Redditch, England, he lives with his wife, two kids, and two chocolate Labs, in San Diego, California.

☺ About PhotoSecrets

👍 Founded in, and online since, 1995.

👍 First color travel photo guides (1997).

👍 First web app photo guides (2012).

👍 First app/book/ebook photo guides (2015).

👍 Largest travel photography database, with over 10,000 locations.

👍 15 color photography books published.

♀ Maps

♀ Map of Taj Mahal

📍 Map of Entrance Forecourt

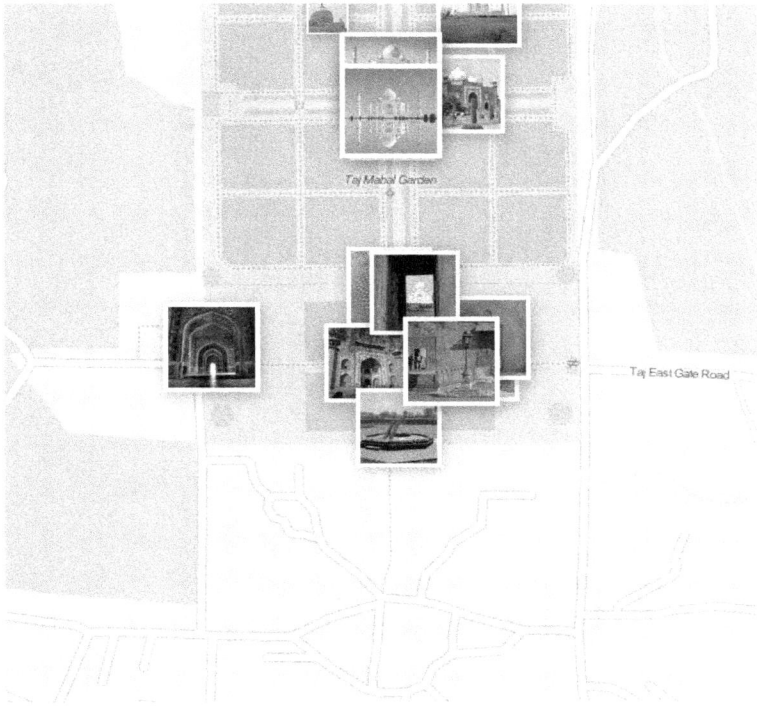

Map of Paradise Garden

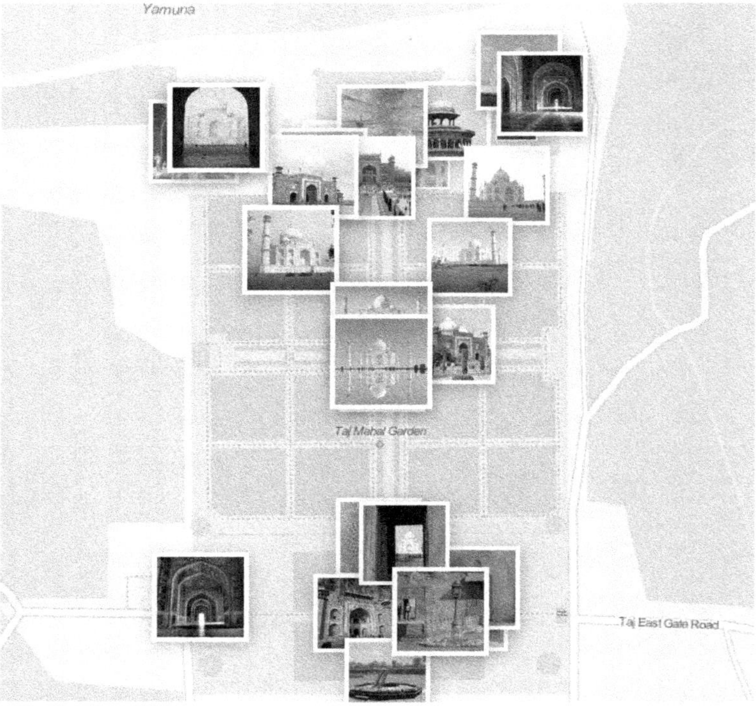

📍 Map of Riverfront Terrace

⚲ Map of Yamuna River

ℹ️ Introduction

👁 At a Glance

At a glance	
ℹ️ **Name:**	Taj Mahal (Arabic for "Crown of Palaces")
🌐 **GPS:**	27.17500, 78.04194
📢 **Fame:**	Masterpiece of world heritage, icon of India
↔ **Far:**	4.4 km (2.75 miles) from the center of Agra
☑ **Web:**	tajmahal.gov.in
🎎 **Opened:**	1653
↕ **Height:**	73 m (240 feet)
🏛 **Style:**	Mughal
Architects:	Ustad Ahmad Lahouri, Ustad Isa
Built by:	Shah Jahan
✉ **Address:**	Agra, Uttar Pradesh 282001, India
Notes:	The Taj Mahal is an extensive complex of buildings and gardens that extends over 22 hectares (55 acres)

ℹ Introduction

THE TAJ MAHAL is an ivory-white marble mausoleum on the south bank of the Yamuna river in the Indian city of Agra. It was commissioned in 1632 by the Mughal emperor, Shah Jahan (reigned 1628–1658), to house the tomb of his favorite wife, Mumtaz Mahal. The tomb is the centrepiece of a 42-acre complex, which includes a mosque and a guest house, and is set in formal gardens bounded on three sides by a crenellated wall.

Construction of the mausoleum was essentially completed in 1643 but work continued on other phases of the project for another 10 years. The Taj Mahal complex is believed to have been completed in its entirety in 1653 at a cost estimated at the time to be around 32 million rupees, which in 2015 would be approximately 52.8 billion rupees (US$827 million). The construction project employed some 20,000 artisans under the guidance of a board of architects led by the court architect to the emperor, Ustad Ahmad Lahauri.

The Taj Mahal was designated as a UNESCO World Heritage Site in 1983 for being "the jewel of Muslim art in India and one of the universally admired masterpieces of the world's heritage." Described by the Nobel laureate, Rabindranath Tagore, as "the tear-drop on the cheek of time," it is regarded by many as the best example of Mughal architecture and a symbol of India's rich history. The Taj Mahal attracts 7–8 million visitors a year. In 2007, it was declared a winner of the New7Wonders of the World (2000–2007) initiative.

—Wikipedia

Views

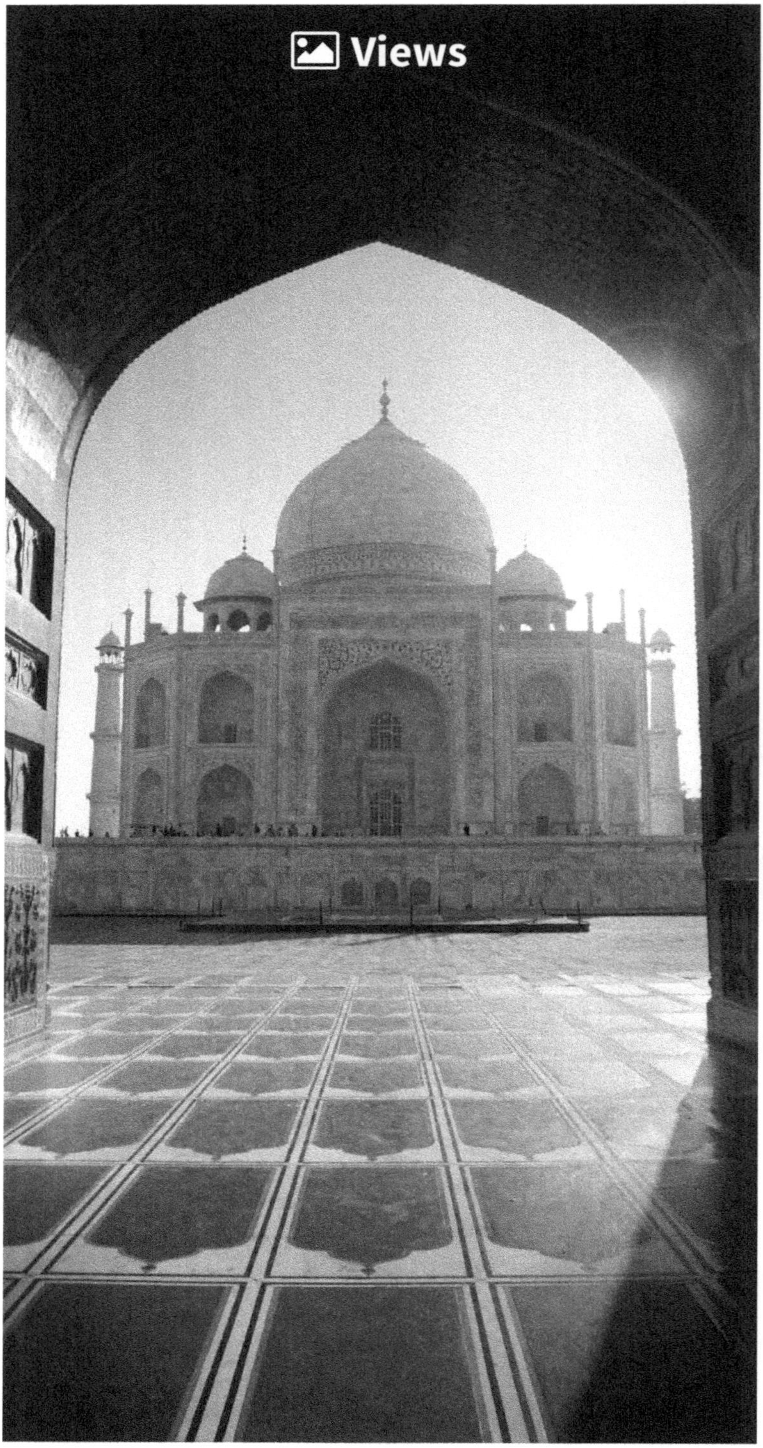

🖼 Great Gate

📍 27.171073, 78.041941 © Sumit Roy/Wikipedia

THE GREAT GATE STANDS TO the north of the entrance forecourt and provides a symbolic transition between the worldly realm of bazaars and caravanserai and the spiritual realm of the paradise garden, mosque and the mausoleum. Its rectangular plan is a variation of the 9-part hasht bihisht plan found in the mausoleum. The corners are articulated with octagonal towers giving the structure a defensive appearance. External domes were reserved for tombs and mosques and so the large central space does not receive any outward expression of its internal dome. From within the great gate, the Mausoleum is framed by the pointed arch of the portal. Inscriptions from the Qu'ran are inlaid around the two northern and southern pishtaqs, the southern one 'Daybreak' invites believers to enter the garden of paradise.—*Wikipedia*

❓ **What:**	Large sandstone gate	◑ **When:**	Afternoon
📍 **Where:**	27.171674,78.042144	📷 **From:**	27.171073, 78.041941
👁 **Look:**	North-northeast	↔ **Far:**	70 m (230 feet)
💬 **AKA:**	Darwaza-i rauza	✉ **Address:**	Taj Mahal, Agra, Uttar Pradesh 282001, India

🖼 East gallery detail

Taj Mahal > Entrance Forecourt > Great Gate

📍 27.171085, 78.042648   © Edmund Gall/Wikipedia

❓ What:	View	🌓 When:	Morning
📍 Where:	27.171642,78.042405	📷 From:	27.171085, 78.042648
👁 Look:	North-northwest	↔ Far:	70 m (220 feet)

✉ **Address:** Taj Mahal, Agra, Uttar Pradesh 282001, India

🖼 Ceiling

Taj Mahal > Entrance Forecourt > Great Gate

📍 27.171685, 78.042129 © Anoop Pushkar/Wikipedia

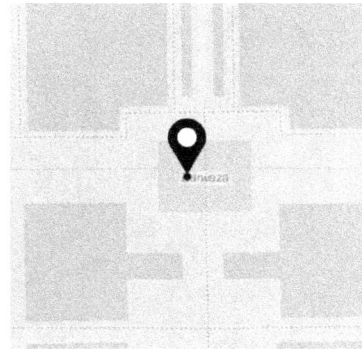

❓ What:	Ceiling	◗ When:	Anytime
📍 Where:	27.171685, 78.042129	✉ Address:	Taj Mahal, Agra, Uttar Pradesh 282001, India

🖼 Framed by doorway

📍 27.171641, 78.042343   © Steve Evans/Wikipedia

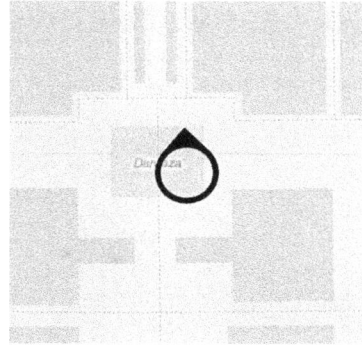

❓ What:	View	◑ When:	Morning
⚲ Where:	27.175002,78.042153	📷 From:	27.171641, 78.042343
👁 Look:	North	↔ Far:	370 m (1230 feet)
✉ Address:	Taj Mahal, Agra, Uttar Pradesh 282001, India		

🖼 East Gate and cloisters

Taj Mahal > Entrance Forecourt

📍 27.171079, 78.042859   © Dennis Jarvis/Wikipedia

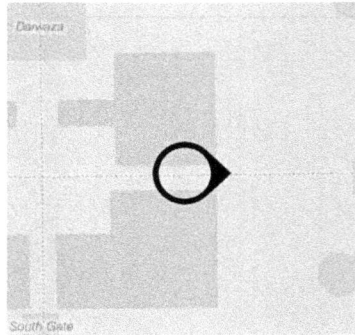

❓ What:	Gate	🌙 When:	Anytime
📍 Where:	27.171076,78.043677	📷 From:	27.171079, 78.042859
👁 Look:	East	↔ Far:	80 m (260 feet)

💬 **AKA:**	Fatehbad Gate	✉ **Address:**	Taj Mahal, Agra, Uttar Pradesh 282001, India

Ideas for East Gate and cloisters

📍 27.202732,78.016662   © Dennis Jarvis/Wikipedia

🖼 East Gate corridor

Taj Mahal > Entrance Forecourt > East Gate and cloisters

📍 27.171275, 78.042934 © Souravita/Wikipedia

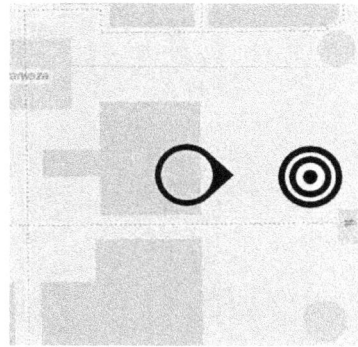

❓ What:	Corridor	◐ When:	Afternoon
📍 Where:	27.171268,78.043487	📷 From:	27.171275, 78.042934
👁 Look:	East	↔ Far:	50 m (180 feet)
✉ Address:	Taj Mahal, Agra, Uttar Pradesh 282001, India		

Ideas for East Gate corridor

© Daljit/Wikipedia

🖼 Interior

Taj Mahal > Entrance Forecourt > West Gate

📍 27.1712, 78.04063   © Sam Hawley/Flickr

❓ **What:**	Interior	🌓 **When:**	Anytime
📍 **Where:**	27.1712, 78.04063	✉ **Address:**	Taj Mahal, Agra, Uttar Pradesh 282001, India

🖼 Entrance well

Taj Mahal > Entrance Forecourt

📍 27.170551, 78.042203   © Manikanta Allam/Wikipedia

❓ What:	Well	🌓 When:	Afternoon
📍 Where:	27.170646,78.042279	📷 From:	27.170551, 78.042203
👁 Look:	Northeast	↔ Far:	12 m (39 feet)
✉ Address:	Taj Mahal, Agra, Uttar Pradesh 282001, India		

🖼 Classic sunrise

Taj Mahal > Paradise Garden > Classic

📍 27.173342, 78.042149   © Seb2583/Shutterstock

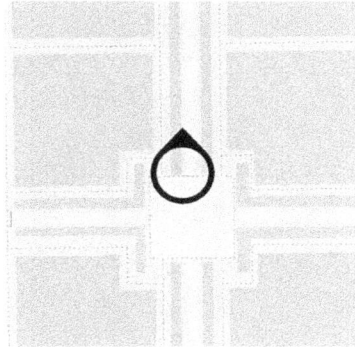

❓ What:	View	◑ When:	Anytime
📍 Where:	27.175002,78.042153	📷 From:	27.173342, 78.042149
👁 Look:	North	↔ Far:	180 m (600 feet)
✉ Address:	Taj Mahal, Agra, Uttar Pradesh 282001, India		

🖼 Classic morning

📍 27.173357, 78.0421412   © Dmitry Strizhakov/Shutterstock

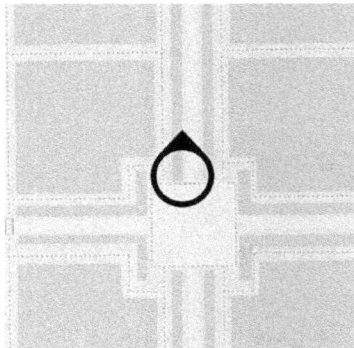

❓ What:	View	◑ When:	Anytime
📍 Where:	27.175002,78.042153	📷 From:	27.173357, 78.0421412

👁 **Look:**	North	↔ **Far:**	180 m (600 feet)
✉ **Address:**	Taj Mahal, Agra, Uttar Pradesh 282001, India		

Ideas for Classic morning

© Olena Tur/Shutterstock

🖼 Reflection

Taj Mahal > Paradise Garden > Classic > Classic morning

📍 27.173099, 78.042143 © Waj/Shutterstock

❓ What:	View	🌓 When:	Anytime
📍 Where:	27.175002,78.042153	📷 From:	27.173099, 78.042143
👁 Look:	North	↔ Far:	210 m (690 feet)

✉ **Address:**	Taj Mahal, Agra, Uttar Pradesh 282001, India

🖼 Classic noon

Taj Mahal > Paradise Garden > Classic

📍 27.173357, 78.0421413   © Marttaelib/Wikipedia

❓ What:	View	◑ When:	Anytime
📍 Where:	27.175002,78.042153	📷 From:	27.173357, 78.0421413

👁 **Look:**	North	↔ **Far:**	180 m (600 feet)
✉ **Address:**	Taj Mahal, Agra, Uttar Pradesh 282001, India		

Ideas for Classic noon

© Vil.sandi/Flickr

🖼 Classic afternoon

Taj Mahal > Paradise Garden > Classic

📍 27.173357, 78.0421414   © RuthChoi/Shutterstock

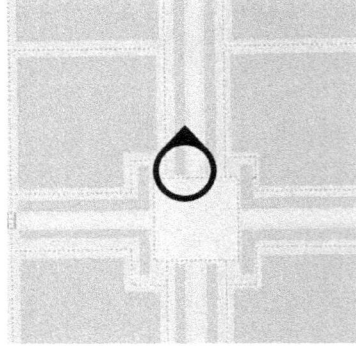

Taj Mahal Garden

❓ **What:**	View	◐ **When:**	Anytime
📍 **Where:**	27.175002,78.042153	📷 **From:**	27.173357, 78.0421414
👁 **Look:**	North	↔ **Far:**	180 m (600 feet)
✉ **Address:**	Taj Mahal, Agra, Uttar Pradesh 282001, India		

Ideas for Classic afternoon

27.173888888889,78.042222222222 © Dhirad/Wikipedia

🖼️ West

Taj Mahal > Paradise Garden > Grass

📍 27.173997, 78.041383   © Ramesh Ng/Wikipedia

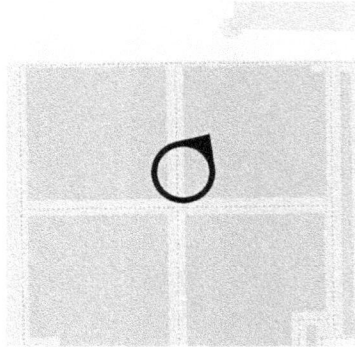

❓ **What:**	View	◑ **When:**	Afternoon
📍 **Where:**	27.175002,78.042153	📷 **From:**	27.173997, 78.041383
👁 **Look:**	Northeast	↔ **Far:**	140 m (440 feet)
✉ **Address:**	Taj Mahal, Agra, Uttar Pradesh 282001, India		

Ideas for West

© Herojit Waikhom/Wikipedia

🖼️ East

Taj Mahal > Paradise Garden > Grass

📍 27.173942, 78.042885

© Aiwok/Wikipedia

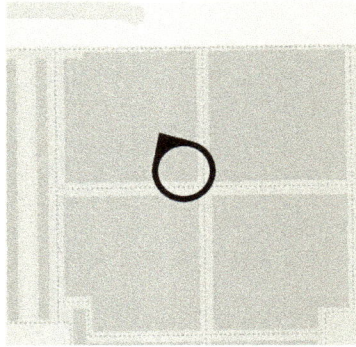

❓ **What:**	View	🌓 **When:**	Anytime
📍 **Where:**	27.175002,78.042153	📷 **From:**	27.173942, 78.042885
👁 **Look:**	North-northwest	↔ **Far:**	140 m (450 feet)
✉ **Address:**	Taj Mahal, Agra, Uttar Pradesh 282001, India		

🖼 Pavilion

Taj Mahal > Paradise Garden

📍 27.1731766, 78.0424104   © Biswarup Ganguly/Wikipedia

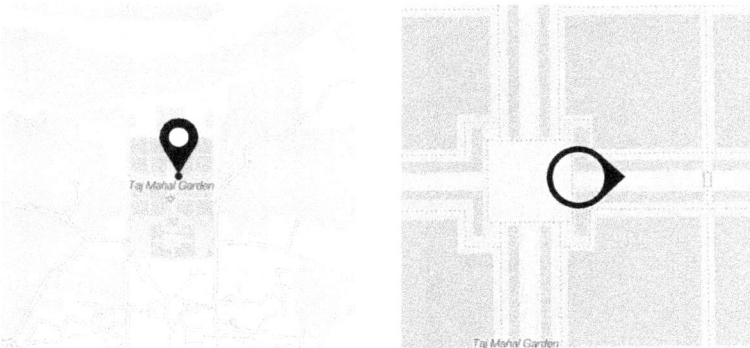

❓ What:	Pavilion	🌓 When:	Afternoon
📍 Where:	27.173188,78.043579	📷 From:	27.1731766, 78.0424104
👁 Look:	East	↔ Far:	120 m (380 feet)
💬 AKA:	Naubat Khana	✉ Address:	Taj Mahal, Agra, Uttar Pradesh 282001, India

🖼 View of View of Great Gate

Taj Mahal > Paradise Garden

📍 27.173018, 78.042155   © Francisco Anzola/Wikipedia

❓ **What:**	View	◑ **When:**	Afternoon
📍 **Where:**	27.171674,78.042144	📷 **From:**	27.173018, 78.042155
👁 **Look:**	South	↔ **Far:**	150 m (490 feet)
✉ **Address:**	Taj Mahal, Agra, Uttar Pradesh 282001, India		

Ideas for View of View of Great Gate

© Wiki-Uk/Wikipedia

🖼 View of View of Mosque

Taj Mahal > Paradise Garden

📍 27.173239, 78.042746   © Francisco Anzola/Wikipedia

❓ **What:**	View	◑ **When:**	Morning
📍 **Where:**	27.174982,78.040701	📷 **From:**	27.173239, 78.042746
👁 **Look:**	Northwest	↔ **Far:**	280 m (920 feet)

✉
Address: Taj Mahal, Agra, Uttar
Pradesh 282001, India

🖼 At sunrise

Taj Mahal > Riverfront Terrace > View

📍 27.175032, 78.043278mad Mahdi Karim Facebook Youtube, Stitching Assisted By/Wikipedia

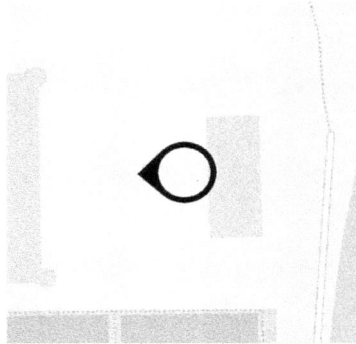

❓ What:	View	◑ When:	Anytime
📍 Where:	27.175002,78.042153	📷 From:	27.175032, 78.043278
👁 Look:	West	↔ Far:	110 m (360 feet)
✉ Address:	Taj Mahal, Agra, Uttar Pradesh 282001, India		

🖼 At morning

📍 27.175441, 78.043297 © Bjørn Christian Tørrissen/Wikipedia

❓ What:	View	🌓 When:	Anytime
📍 Where:	27.175002,78.042153	📷 From:	27.175441, 78.043297
👁 Look:	West-southwest	↔ Far:	120 m (400 feet)
✉ Address:	Taj Mahal, Agra, Uttar Pradesh 282001, India		

🖼 At afternoon

Taj Mahal > Riverfront Terrace > View

📍 27.174517, 78.043193   © Tanweer Morshed/Wikipedia

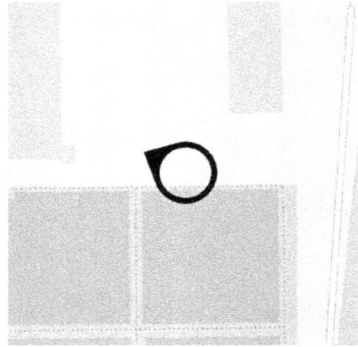

❓ **What:**	View	◑ **When:**	Morning
📍 **Where:**	27.175002,78.042153	📷 **From:**	27.174517, 78.043193
👁 **Look:**	West-northwest	↔ **Far:**	120 m (380 feet)
✉ **Address:**	Taj Mahal, Agra, Uttar Pradesh 282001, India		

Ideas for at afternoon

© Narendra577502/Wikipedia

© Archishilpi14/Wikipedia

🖼 Close corner

Taj Mahal > Riverfront Terrace > View > Close

📍 27.174645, 78.042543 © Umesh Namdeo/Wikipedia

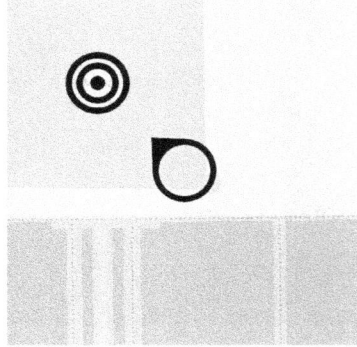

❓ **What:**	View	◐ **When:**		Morning
📍 **Where:**	27.175002,78.042153	📷 **From:**		27.174645, 78.042543
👁 **Look:**	Northwest	↔ **Far:**		60 m (180 feet)
✉ **Address:**	Taj Mahal, Agra, Uttar Pradesh 282001, India			

Ideas for Close corner

© Rahul Jain/Wikipedia

⛰ Close corner sunset

Taj Mahal > Riverfront Terrace > View > Close > Close corner

📍 27.174647, 78.041645

© Rusticus80/Flickr

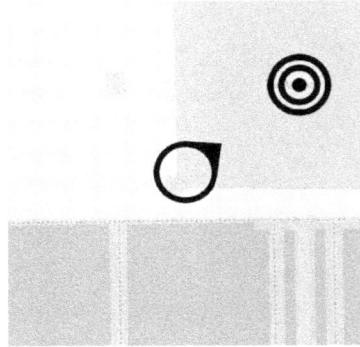

❓ **What:**	View	◑ **When:**	Anytime
📍 **Where:**	27.175002,78.042153	📷 **From:**	27.174647, 78.041645
👁 **Look:**	Northeast	↔ **Far:**	60 m (210 feet)
✉ **Address:**	Taj Mahal, Agra, Uttar Pradesh 282001, India		

🖼 Close side

Taj Mahal > Riverfront Terrace > View > Close

📍 27.174682, 78.042183 © Anoop Pushkar/Wikipedia

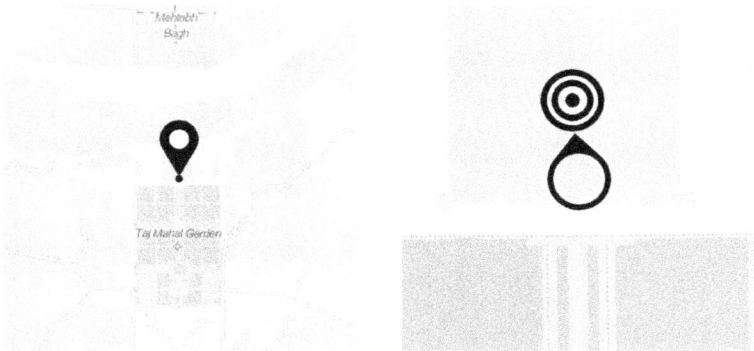

❓ What:	View	🌓 When:	Morning
📍 Where:	27.175002,78.042153	📷 From:	27.174682, 78.042183
👁 Look:	North	↔ Far:	40 m (110 feet)
✉ Address:	Taj Mahal, Agra, Uttar Pradesh 282001, India		

Ideas for Close side

© Guptaele/Wikipedia

© Guptaele/Wikipedia

© Arpit Jawa/Wikipedia

© Piyush Kumar/Flickr

🖼 Close top

Taj Mahal > Riverfront Terrace > View > Close

📍 27.1738846, 78.041611　　　　　　　© Biswarup Ganguly/Wikipedia

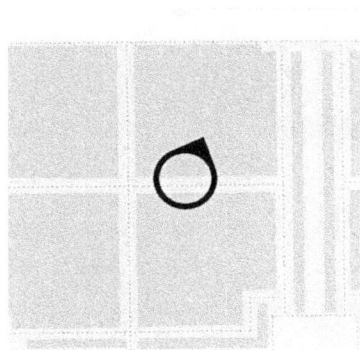

❓ **What:**	View	◑ **When:**	Afternoon
📍 **Where:**	27.175002,78.042153	📷 **From:**	27.1738846, 78.041611
👁 **Look:**	North-northeast	↔ **Far:**	140 m (440 feet)
✉ **Address:**	Taj Mahal, Agra, Uttar Pradesh 282001, India		

Ideas for Close top

© Tor/Wikipedia

🖼️ Details art

Taj Mahal > Riverfront Terrace > Tomb > Details

📍 27.174883, 78.041810   © Anoop Pushkar/Wikipedia

❓ What:	Detail	🕐 When:	Anytime
📍 Where:	27.174883, 78.041810	✉️ Address:	Taj Mahal, Agra, Uttar Pradesh 282001, India

Ideas for Details art

© Rajacommonswiki/Wikipedia

© Maahmaah/Wikipedia

🖼 Details inlay

Taj Mahal > Riverfront Terrace > Tomb > Details

📍 27.174729, 78.041835   © Teufel1987/Wikipedia

❓ What:	Detail	🌓 When:	Anytime
📍 Where:	27.174729, 78.041835	✉ Address:	Taj Mahal, Agra, Uttar Pradesh 282001, India

🖼 Tombs in crypt

Taj Mahal > Riverfront Terrace > Tomb > Details

📍 27.174996, 78.042149   © Donelson/Wikipedia

❓ What:	View	🌓 When:	Anytime
📍 Where:	27.174996, 78.042149	✉ Address:	Taj Mahal, Agra, Uttar Pradesh 282001, India

Ttombs of Mumtaz Mahal and Shah Jahan in the lower level.

🖼 Interior

Taj Mahal > Riverfront Terrace > Mosque

📍 27.174874, 78.040564   © Samir Luther/Flickr

❷ What:	Interior	◑ When:	Anytime
♀ Where:	27.174874, 78.040564	✉ Address:	Taj Mahal, Agra, Uttar Pradesh 282001, India

🖼 Framed arch

Taj Mahal > Riverfront Terrace > Mosque

📍 27.174983, 78.040789 © Jool-yan/Shutterstock

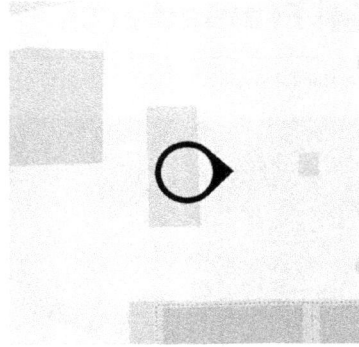

❓ **What:**	View	◑ **When:**	Anytime
📍 **Where:**	27.175002,78.042153	📷 **From:**	27.174983, 78.040789
👁 **Look:**	East	↔ **Far:**	130 m (440 feet)
✉ **Address:**	Taj Mahal, Agra, Uttar Pradesh 282001, India		

Ideas for Framed arch

© Matt Paish/Flickr

🖼 Framed arch silhouette

Taj Mahal > Riverfront Terrace > Mosque > Framed arch

📍 27.174985, 78.040752   © Achim Baque/Shutterstock

❓ What:	View	◐ When:	Sunset
📍 Where:	27.175002,78.042153	📷 From:	27.174985, 78.040752
👁 Look:	East	↔ Far:	140 m (450 feet)
✉ Address:	Taj Mahal, Agra, Uttar Pradesh 282001, India		

Ideas for Framed arch silhouette

© Diego Delso/ Wikipedia

© Labrasevic/Wikipedia

© Clément Bardot/ Wikipedia

🖼️ Photographer

Taj Mahal > Riverfront Terrace > Mosque > Framed arch > Framed arch silhouette

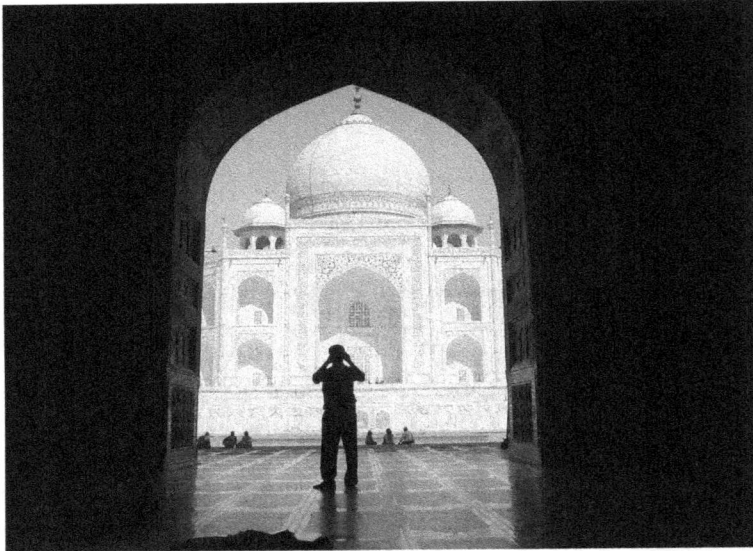

📍 27.174990, 78.040720   © Ankushsharma2002/Wikipedia

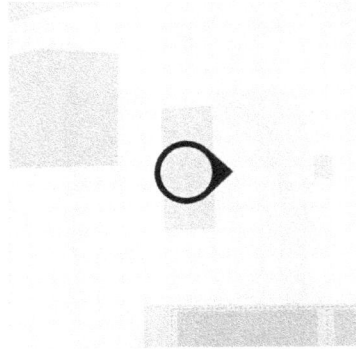

❓ **What:**	View	🌓 **When:**	Afternoon
📍 **Where:**	27.175002,78.042153	📷 **From:**	27.174990, 78.040720
👁 **Look:**	East	↔ **Far:**	140 m (460 feet)
✉ **Address:**	Taj Mahal, Agra, Uttar Pradesh 282001, India		

🖼️ Interior

Taj Mahal > Riverfront Terrace > Jawab

📍 27.175255, 78.043492   © Bjørn Christian Tørrissen/Wikipedia

❓ What:	Interior	🌓 When:	Anytime
📍 Where:	27.175255, 78.043492	✉️ Address:	Taj Mahal, Agra, Uttar Pradesh 282001, India

Ideas for Interior

© Kiranmidigeshi/Wikipedia

© Adrianne Wadewitz /Wikipedia

🖼 View of View of Great Gate

Taj Mahal > Riverfront Terrace

📍 27.174578, 78.042046

© Airknight/Wikipedia

❓ **What:**	View	◐ **When:**	Afternoon
📍 **Where:**	27.171674,78.042144	📷 **From:**	27.174578, 78.042046
👁 **Look:**	South	↔ **Far:**	320 m (1060 feet)
✉ **Address:**	Taj Mahal, Agra, Uttar Pradesh 282001, India		

Ideas for View of View of Great Gate

© Diego Delso/Wikipedia

🖼 View of View of Mosque

Taj Mahal > Riverfront Terrace

📍 27.174588, 78.041568

© Manav/Wikipedia

❓ **What:**	View	◑ **When:**	Morning
📍 **Where:**	27.174982,78.040701	📷 **From:**	27.174588, 78.041568
👁 **Look:**	West-northwest	↔ **Far:**	100 m (310 feet)
✉ **Address:**	Taj Mahal, Agra, Uttar Pradesh 282001, India		

🖼 View of northwest octagonal tower

Taj Mahal > Riverfront Terrace

📍 27.175035, 78.0426998   © Biswarup Ganguly/Wikipedia

❓ What:	View	◐ When:	Afternoon
📍 Where:	27.175520,78.043545	📷 From:	27.175035, 78.0426998
👁 Look:	East-northeast	↔ Far:	100 m (320 feet)
✉ Address:	Taj Mahal, Agra, Uttar Pradesh 282001, India		

🖼 River northeast sunrise

Taj Mahal > Yamuna > River > River northeast

📍 27.177748, 78.044262   © Rawpixel/Shutterstock

❓ What:	View	◑ When:	Anytime
📍 Where:	27.175002,78.042153	📷 From:	27.177748, 78.044262
👁 Look:	Southwest	↔ Far:	370 m (1210 feet)
✉ Address:	Taj Mahal, Agra, Uttar Pradesh 282001, India		

Ideas for River northeast sunrise

© Pius Lee/Shutterstock

🖼 River northeast sunset

Taj Mahal > Yamuna > River > River northeast

📍 27.177748, 78.0442622 © Travel & Shit/Wikipedia

❓ **What:**	View	◑ **When:**	Anytime
📍 **Where:**	27.175002,78.042153	📷 **From:**	27.177748, 78.0442622
👁 **Look:**	Southwest	↔ **Far:**	370 m (1210 feet)
✉ **Address:**	Taj Mahal, Agra, Uttar Pradesh 282001, India		

🖼 River northeast boat

📍 27.176884, 78.043913 © Saidur/Wikipedia

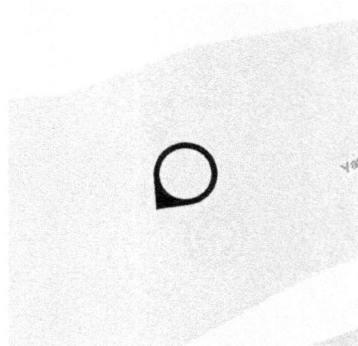

❓ **What:**	View	◑ **When:**	Morning
📍 **Where:**	27.175002,78.042153	📷 **From:**	27.176884, 78.043913
👁 **Look:**	Southwest	↔ **Far:**	270 m (890 feet)
✉ **Address:**	Taj Mahal, Agra, Uttar Pradesh 282001, India		

🖼️ River northeast bike

Taj Mahal > Yamuna > River > River northeast

📍 27.177352, 78.042626   © Leigh Harries/Wikipedia

❓ What:	View	◑ When:	Anytime
📍 Where:	27.175002,78.042153	📷 From:	27.177352, 78.042626
👁️ Look:	South	↔ Far:	270 m (870 feet)
✉️ Address:	Taj Mahal, Agra, Uttar Pradesh 282001, India		

🖼 River north vertical

Taj Mahal > Yamuna > River > River north

📍 27.177214, 78.042068   © Leigh Harries/Wikipedia

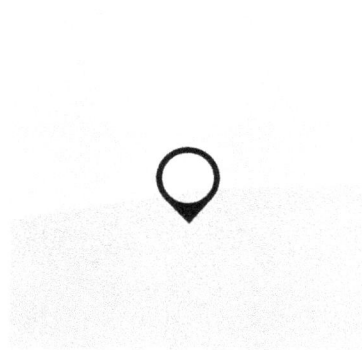

What:	View	When:	Afternoon
Where:	27.175002,78.042153	From:	27.177214, 78.042068
Look:	South	Far:	250 m (810 feet)
Address:	Taj Mahal, Agra, Uttar Pradesh 282001, India		

🖼️ River north sunset

📍 27.177214, 78.042068   © Nedim chaabene/Flickr

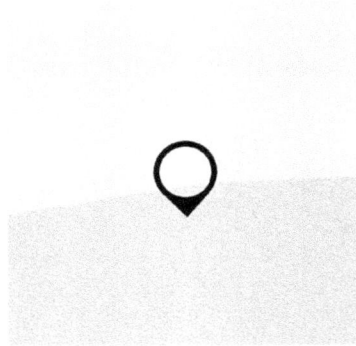

❓ What:	View	◐ When:	Afternoon
📍 Where:	27.175002,78.042153	📷 From:	27.177214, 78.042068
👁 Look:	South	↔ Far:	250 m (810 feet)
✉ Address:	Taj Mahal, Agra, Uttar Pradesh 282001, India		

🖼 River northwest dawn

Taj Mahal > Yamuna > River > River northwest

📍 27.178159, 78.039912   © Koshy Koshy/Wikipedia

❓ **What:**	View	◑ **When:**	Anytime
📍 **Where:**	27.175002,78.042153	📷 **From:**	27.178159, 78.039912
👁 **Look:**	South-southeast	↔ **Far:**	420 m (1360 feet)
✉ **Address:**	Taj Mahal, Agra, Uttar Pradesh 282001, India		

![icon] River northwest afternoon

Taj Mahal > Yamuna > River > River northwest

📍 27.177155, 78.040770

© Someone/Wikipedia

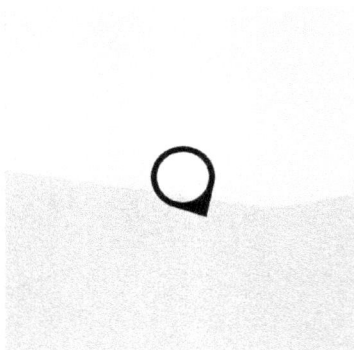

❓ What:	View	◐ When:	Anytime
📍 Where:	27.175002,78.042153	📷 From:	27.177155, 78.040770
👁 Look:	South-southeast	↔ Far:	280 m (900 feet)
✉ Address:	Taj Mahal, Agra, Uttar Pradesh 282001, India		

Ideas for River northwest afternoon

© E/Wikipedia

© Tor/Wikipedia

![icon] Cows

Taj Mahal > Yamuna > River > River northwest > River northwest afternoon

📍 27.177613, 78.040904

© Dcastor/Wikipedia

❓ **What:**	View	◑ **When:**	Anytime
📍 **Where:**	27.175002,78.042153	📷 **From:**	27.177613, 78.040904
👁 **Look:**	South-southeast	↔ **Far:**	320 m (1030 feet)
✉ **Address:**	Taj Mahal, Agra, Uttar Pradesh 282001, India		

🖼️ River northwest sunset

Taj Mahal > Yamuna > River > River northwest

📍 27.177147, 78.040647

© Boris Stroujko/Shutterstock

❓ **What:**	View	◑ **When:**	Anytime
📍 **Where:**	27.175002,78.042153	📷 **From:**	27.177147, 78.040647
👁 **Look:**	South-southeast	↔ **Far:**	280 m (920 feet)
✉ **Address:**	Taj Mahal, Agra, Uttar Pradesh 282001, India		

Ideas for River northwest sunset

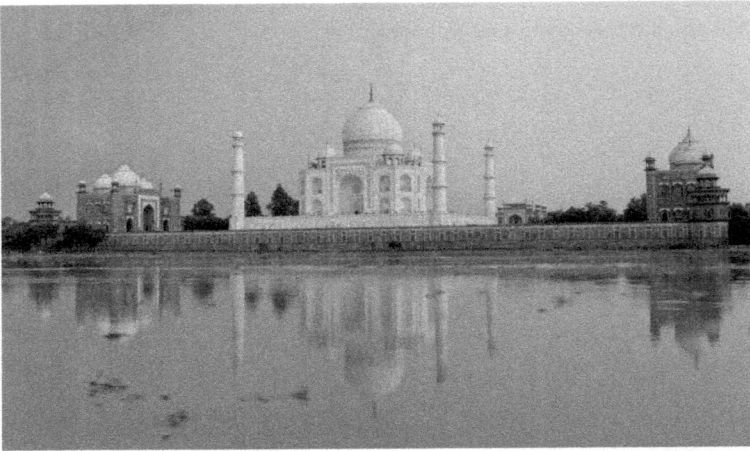

© Boris Stroujko/Shutterstock

🖼️ River northwest at dusk

Taj Mahal > Yamuna > River > River northwest

📍 27.177147, 78.0406471 © Boris Stroujko/Shutterstock

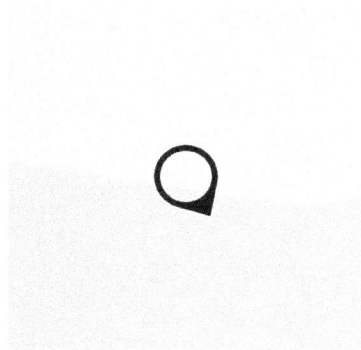

❓ **What:**	View	🌓 **When:**	Anytime
📍 **Where:**	27.175002,78.042153	📷 **From:**	27.177147, 78.0406471
👁 **Look:**	South-southeast	↔ **Far:**	280 m (920 feet)
✉ **Address:**	Taj Mahal, Agra, Uttar Pradesh 282001, India		

Ideas for River northwest at dusk

© Kewal Somani/Wikipedia

🖼 Moonlight Garden

Taj Mahal

📍 27.180092, 78.042026   © :aks Khandelwal/Wikipedia

MEHTAB BAGH is a charbagh complex in Agra, North India. It lies north of the Taj Mahal complex and the Agra Fort on the opposite side of the Yamuna River, in the flood plains. The garden complex, square in shape, measures about 300 by 300 metres (980 ft × 980 ft) and is perfectly aligned with the Taj Mahal on the opposite bank. During the rainy season, the ground becomes partially flooded.

   —Wikipedia

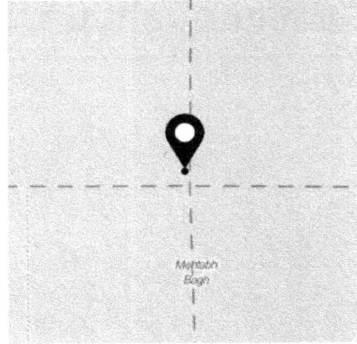

❓ What:	Mughal-era gardens	🕐 When:	Anytime
📍 Where:	27.180092, 78.042026	💬 AKA:	Mehtab Bagh
✉ Address:	Mehtab Bagh, near Taj Mahal, Nagla Devjit, Agra, Uttar Pradesh 282001, India		

![] View

Taj Mahal > Moonlight Garden

📍 27.180064, 78.042028   © Narender9/Wikipedia

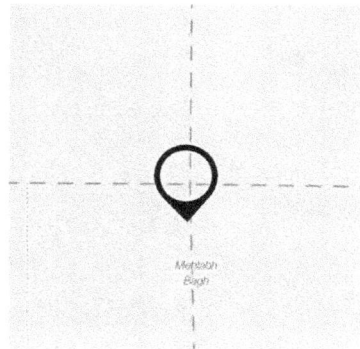

❓ What:	Mughal-era gardens	◑ When:	Anytime
📍 Where:	27.175002,78.042153	📷 From:	27.180064, 78.042028
👁 Look:	South	↔ Far:	0.56 km (0.35 miles)
✉ Address:	Mehtab Bagh, near Taj Mahal, Nagla Devjit, Agra, Uttar Pradesh 282001, India		

🖼 From Agra Fort

Taj Mahal

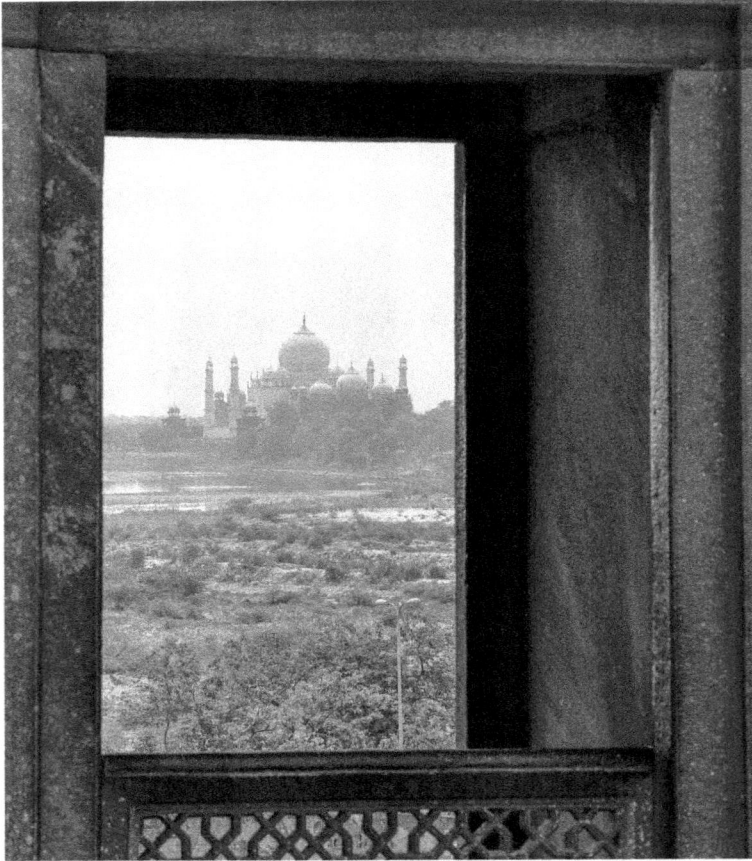

📍 27.176888, 78.023612

© Louen/Wikipedia

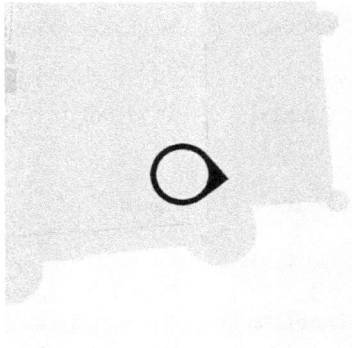

❷ What:	View	◑ When:	Afternoon
⚲ Where:	27.175002,78.042153	📷 From:	27.176888, 78.023612
👁 Look:	East	↔ Far:	1.85 km (1.15 miles)
✉ Address:	Taj Mahal, Agra, Uttar Pradesh 282001, India		

▪▪ Index

A

About PhotoSecrets 13
Author 12

B

Body matter
- Views 22
Books by PhotoSecrets 13
Building
- Jawab 77

C

Ceiling 27
Char Bagh 37
Classic 37
Classic afternoon 44
Classic morning 38
- Reflection 40
Classic noon 42
Classic sunrise 37
Classic
- afternoon 44
- morning 38
- noon 42
- sunrise 37
Close 58
Close corner 58
Close corner sunset 60
Close corner
- sunset 60
Close side 61
Close top 63
Close
- corner 58

- side 61
- top 63
Contents 8
Copyright page 6
Corridor
- East Gate corridor 32
Courtyard
- Entrance Forecourt 23
Cows 94

D

Darwaza-i rauza 23
Detail
- Details art 65
- Details inlay 67
Details 65
Details art 65
Details inlay 67
Details
- art 65
- inlay 67
- Tombs in crypt 68
Disclaimer 6
Dusk
- River northwest 97

E

East 48
East gallery detail 25
East Gate and cloisters 30
- East Gate corridor 32
East Gate corridor 32
Entrance Forecourt 23
- East Gate and cloisters 30
- Entrance well 36
- Great Gate 23

- map 15
- West Gate 35
Entrance well 36

F

Fatehbad Gate 30
Fatehpuri 35
Flickr 6
Foreword 9
Framed arch 71
Framed arch silhouette 74
- Photographer 76
Framed arch
- silhouette 74
Framed by doorway 28
From Agra Fort 102
Front matter 2
- Introduction 19
- Maps 14

G

Gallery 2
Gallery by Rank 2
Gallery by Time 3
Gallery
- by Rank 2
- by Time 3
Garden
- Moonlight Garden 99
- Paradise Garden 37
Gate
- East Gate and cloisters 30
- Great Gate 23
- West Gate 35
Glance 19
Grass 46

- East 48
- West 46
Great Gate 23
- Ceiling 27
- East gallery detail 25
- Framed by doorway 28

H
Hudson, Andrew 12

I
Interior 35, 69, 77
Introduction 19, 20
- at a Glance 19
- Introduction 20

J
Jawab 77
- Interior 77
Jilaukhana 23

K
Krist, Bob 10

M
Map of Entrance Forecourt 15
Map of Paradise Garden 16
Map of Riverfront Terrace 17
Map of Taj Mahal 14
Map of Yamuna River 18
MapQuest 6
Maps 14
- Map of Entrance Forecourt 15
- Map of Paradise Garden 16
- Map of Riverfront Terrace 17
- Map of Taj Mahal 14
- Map of Yamuna River 18
Mehman Khana 77

Mehtab Bagh 99
Moonlight Garden 99
- View 101
Mosque 69
- Framed arch 71
- Interior 69

N
Naubat Khana 49

O
OpenStreetMap 6

P
Paradise Garden 37
- Classic 37
- Grass 46
- map 16
- Pavilion 49
- View of View of Great Gate 50
- View of View of Mosque 52
Pavilion 49
Photographer 76
PhotoSecrets 13

R
Rauza-i munauwara 65
Reflection 40
River 83
River north 88
River north sunset 90
River north vertical 88
River north
- sunset 90
- vertical 88
River northeast 83
River northeast bike 87

River northeast boat 86
River northeast sunrise 83
River northeast sunset 85
River northeast
- bike 87
- boat 86
- sunrise 83
- sunset 85
River northwest 91
River northwest afternoon 92
- Cows 94
River northwest dawn 91
River northwest sunset 95
River northwest
- afternoon 92
- at dusk 97
- dawn 91
- sunset 95
River
- north 88
- northeast 83
- northwest 91
- Yamuna 83
Riverfront Terrace 54
- Jawab 77
- map 17
- Mosque 69
- Tomb 65
- View 54
- View of northwest octagonal tower 82
- View of View of Great Gate 79
- View of View of Mosque 81

S

Shutterstock 6

T

Table of Contents 8
Taj Mahal
- Entrance Forecourt 23
- from Agra Fort 102
- map 14
- Moonlight Garden 99
- Paradise Garden 37
- Riverfront Terrace 54
- Yamuna 83
Terrace
- Riverfront Terrace 54
Tomb 65
- Details 65
Tombs in crypt 68

V

View 54, 101
View of northwest octagonal tower 82
View of View of Great Gate 50, 79
View of View of Mosque 52, 81
Views 22
- Classic 37
- Close 58
- Details 65
- Grass 46
- River 83
- River north 88
- River northeast 83
- River northwest 91
- View 54

W

Welcome 11
Well
- Entrance well 36

West 46
West Gate 35
- Interior 35
Wikimedia 6
Wikipedia 6

Y

Yamuna 83
Yamuna River
- map 18
Yamuna
- River 83

📣 More Acclaim for PhotoSecrets

"Tips to make that perfect picture on your next trip."
—National Geographic Traveler

"Outstanding. Well written, well researched, well designed and well produced. I wish it had been my idea!"
—Robert Holmes, professional travel photographer

"PhotoSecrets books are the guidebooks I consult for personal as well as my company's photo travel."
—Joe Van Os, Joseph Van Os Photo Safaris

A "photographer's dream."
—San Jose Mercury News

"Highly recommended."
—Shutterbug

"Detailed maps on where and when to capture the best and most unique shots."
—Endless Vacation

"Gives all kinds of useful tips."
—Photo Technique

"Cleverly designed maps, superb photographs, this is magnificent."
—John Clayton, KKGO Radio

"You'll learn a lot about photography, even if you're just an armchair traveler."
—Family Photo

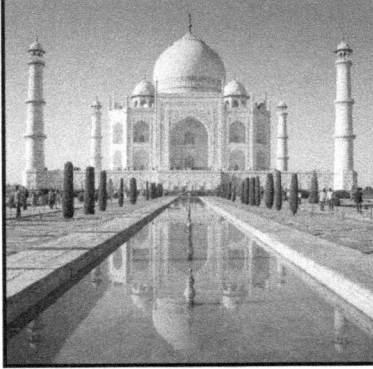

PhotoSecrets

TAJ MAHAL

www.ingramcontent.com/pod-product-compliance
Lightning Source LLC
Chambersburg PA
CBHW032140040426
42449CB00005B/337